# CAPE DISAPPOINTMENT LIGHT

## The First Lighthouse in the Pacific Northwest

**AILEEN WEINTRAUB**

The Rosen Publishing Group's
PowerKids Press™
New York

*To Melissa, for being there through all of life's joys and disappointments*

Published in 2003 by The Rosen Publishing Group, Inc.
29 East 21st Street, New York, NY 10010

First Edition

Editors: Leslie Kaplan and Jennifer Landau
Book Design: Maria E. Melendez

Photo credits: Cover photo and inset, title page photo, p. 4, p. 9 top right, p. 14 top left, p. 16, p. 17 top right, p. 19, p. 22 bottom right © United States Lighthouse Society; p. 5 top right © Richard T. Nowitz/CORBIS; p. 7 © Wolfgang Kaehler/CORBIS; p. 8 © CORBIS; p. 10 top left © Bettmann/CORBIS; p. 11 © Layne Kennedy/CORBIS; p. 12 © Lowell Georgia/CORBIS; p. 15 © Richard Cummins/CORBIS; p. 20 David Muench/CORBIS; cover, title page, backgrounds, and border illustrations by Maria Melendez.

Weintraub, Aileen, 1973–
       Cape Disappointment Light : the first lighthouse in the Pacific Northwest / Aileen Weintraub. — 1st ed.
          p. cm. — (Great lighthouses of North America)
       Includes bibliographical references and index.
       Summary: A history of the lighthouse that sits on a high cliff overlooking the Columbia River in Ilwaco, Washington.
       ISBN 0-8239-6172-9 (library binding)
       1. Cape Disappointment Lighthouse (Wash.)—Juvenile literature. [1. Cape Disappointment Lighthouse (Wash.) 2. Lighthouses.]   I. Title. II. Series: Weintraub, Aileen, 1973–    . Great lighthouses of North America.
VK1025.C25W45 2003
387.1'55'09792—dc21

2001003897

# Contents

*1* Guiding Ships     *5*

*2* Rocky Coastline, Dangerous Waves     *6*

*3* Naming the Cape     *9*

*4* Westward Expansion     *10*

*5* The *Oriole* Sinks     *13*

*6* The Lighthouse Is Completed     *14*

*7* Shining the Light     *17*

*8* Stories of the Lighthouse Keepers     *18*

*9* The Graveyard of the Pacific     *21*

*10* Cape Disappointment Light Still Shines     *22*

Glossary     *23*

Index     *24*

Web Sites     *24*

Cape Disappointment Light sits on a steep, granite cliff on the southwestern tip of Washington state.

# Guiding Ships

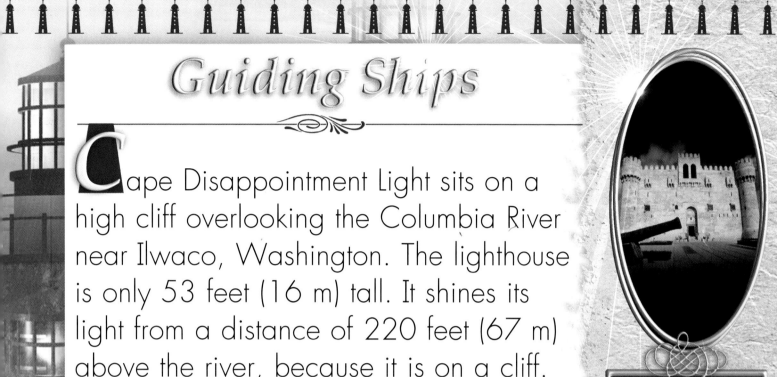

Cape Disappointment Light sits on a high cliff overlooking the Columbia River near Ilwaco, Washington. The lighthouse is only 53 feet (16 m) tall. It shines its light from a distance of 220 feet (67 m) above the river, because it is on a cliff. A lighthouse is a tower with a bright light at the top. This light helps to guide ships through rough seas. Lighthouses have been used since **ancient** times. The first lighthouse was named Pharos. It was built in the **port** city of Alexandria, Egypt, between 290 B.C. and 270 B.C. Cape Disappointment, also known as Cape D, is the oldest lighthouse in the Pacific Northwest. It remains an active lighthouse.

This is the fort where Pharos, the lighthouse of Alexandria, once stood.

5

# Rocky Coastline, Dangerous Waves

Cape Disappointment Light was built to overlook the Columbia River for an important reason. The Columbia River is one of the most **treacherous** bodies of water in the world. There is a dangerous sandbar where this river meets the Pacific Ocean. A sandbar is sand that rises from the ocean floor, which may not be visible above the water. Ship captains usually cannot see sandbars. If the captains do not know that a sandbar is there, the ships might crash.

Cape Disappointment often has bad weather. Terrible storms cause rising ocean waves. The area is also one of the foggiest on the West Coast. Once fog sets in, it is impossible to see. Before a lighthouse was built at Cape Disappointment, hundreds of ships crashed along its rocky coastline.

*Cape Disappointment Light is often somewhat cloaked, or hidden, by fog.*
*Fog is a cloud at Earth's surface.*

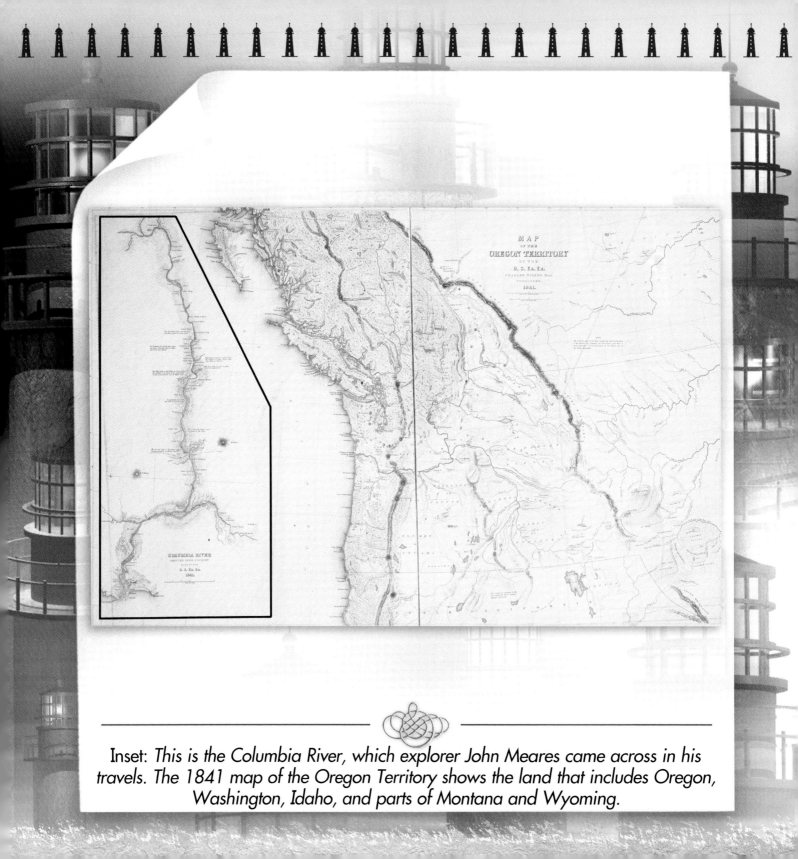

Inset: *This is the Columbia River, which explorer John Meares came across in his travels. The 1841 map of the Oregon Territory shows the land that includes Oregon, Washington, Idaho, and parts of Montana and Wyoming.*

# Naming the Cape

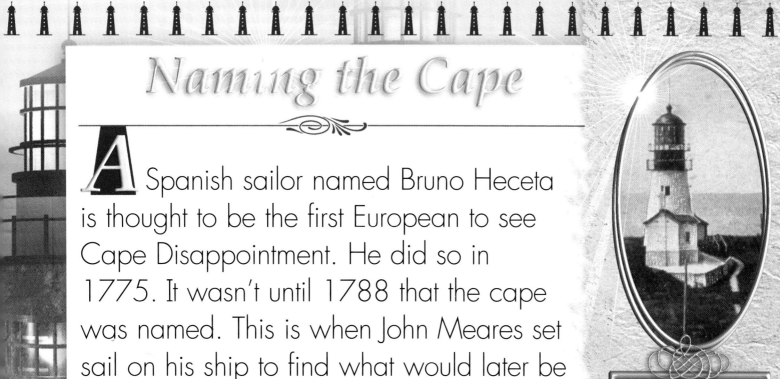

A Spanish sailor named Bruno Heceta is thought to be the first European to see Cape Disappointment. He did so in 1775. It wasn't until 1788 that the cape was named. This is when John Meares set sail on his ship to find what would later be called the Columbia River. Meares was a British fur trader. He wanted to locate new **routes** to make trading by sea faster and easier. He came upon the entrance of the Columbia River but didn't realize it. The entrance looked shallow, and Meares did not think it was worth sailing into. He doubted this was the river for which he was searching. Sad that his mission had failed, he named the area Cape Disappointment.

Cape D is one of the oldest surviving structures on the Pacific Northwest coast.

# Westward Expansion

People traveling west by land rode in covered wagons, often by a route called the Oregon Trail.

**B**y 1848, trade was increasing in the western United States. Gold had been found in California, and people went there to make their fortunes. Around that time, **Congress** created the Oregon Territory. This was land that stretched through what are now the states of Oregon, Washington, Idaho, and parts of Montana and Wyoming. With so many people traveling to the West Coast, a need arose for safe **navigation**. Building lighthouses along the coastline would help trade ships to travel more safely through the waters of the West Coast. The U.S. government sent **surveyors** to find eight places where lighthouses were most needed. One site the surveyors chose was Cape Disappointment.

Left: *Scotts Bluff is a tall cliff that was used as a landmark by pioneers traveling on the Oregon Trail.* Right: *This is a model of a covered wagon used by pioneers.*

There are strong waves at the Columbia River entrance to the Pacific Ocean.
Today the U.S. Coast Guard watches these waters, ready to rescue ships in need.

# The Oriole Sinks

Construction of Cape Disappointment Light was supposed to start in 1853. A ship called the *Oriole* was responsible for bringing materials to the site. During this time, there was poor weather along the coast. The *Oriole* waited eight days at sea before trying to pass the dangerous sandbar that connects the Columbia River to the Pacific Ocean. On September 13, 1853, the *Oriole's* crew attempted to steer the ship across the sandbar. Suddenly the wind died down. The strong **current** pulled the ship across some rocks. The bottom of the boat split open. None of the crew members drowned, but all the materials for the lighthouse sank. The ship went down only 2 miles (3 km) from the site where construction of Cape D was to begin.

# The Lighthouse Is Completed

Cape Disappointment Light, built in the Cape Cod style, has a single-story home next to a tower.

The stone tower for Cape Disappointment Light was completed in the fall of 1856. The lighthouse was painted with a black stripe to make it easier to see during the day against the light sky and the dark trees. This stripe makes the lighthouse a **daymarker**. Cape D is the only West Coast lighthouse that is a daymarker. A fog bell weighing 1,600 pounds (726 kg) was **installed** in the lighthouse. When fog grew too thick for the light to shine through, this bell was rung every 10 seconds. At times the wind and the waves were so loud that even the fog bell couldn't be heard. Today it is no longer in use.

14

*As night approaches, you can see both the glowing lantern of Cape Disappointment Light and the stripe that makes it a daymarker.*

*This is a lantern room containing a Fresnel lens. The original lantern room at Cape D was not big enough to hold a Fresnel lens and had to be rebuilt.*

# Shining the Light

The shining light at Cape D was a fixed, steady beam. The lighthouse originally had a first **order** Fresnel lens. Later a fourth order Fresnel lens replaced it. Frenchman Augustin Fresnel invented the Fresnel lens in 1822. This lens comes in six sizes. The first order is the most powerful and shines the brightest. The lens looks like a beehive and is made up of hundreds of pieces of glass. The lens takes all the rays of light and bends them into a single beam. The light at Cape Disappointment originally used 18 **wicks** and needed 5 gallons (19 l) of oil each night. It shone at 80,000 **candlepower**. This is equal to the brightness of 80,000 candles.

The original Fresnel lens of Cape D is on display at the Lewis and Clark Interpretive Center.

# Stories of the Lighthouse Keepers

Keepers at Cape Disappointment had very hard jobs. They had to make sure the light worked properly. They also kept a close lookout for ships in **distress**. In 1860, Keeper Joel Munson was upset by recent shipwrecks and wanted to raise money for a lifesaving boat. He hosted square dances at which he played the fiddle and charged a small entrance fee.

In the late 1800s, George Esterbrook, an assistant keeper at Cape D, was cleaning the tower on a stormy night when he locked himself out on the **balcony**. He had to climb a long, copper lightning **rod** to get back inside. A few weeks later, he quit his job. Esterbrook went on to study medicine and became a doctor.

*Here we see a keeper on his daily rounds. Lighthouse keepers wrote their observations in logbooks to record what took place on their watches.*

Since 1856, Cape Disappointment Light has guided ships through the part of the Columbia River known as the Graveyard of the Pacific.

# The Graveyard of the Pacific

The Columbia River was given the nickname the Graveyard of the Pacific because so many ships have crashed there. One such ship was the *Strathblane*. On November 3, 1891, the *Strathblane* became **stranded** on the sandbar. The keepers at Cape Disappointment tried to help. Their lifeboat was overturned by the waves, and they had to turn back. The keepers tried again to reach the ship, but they could not. Eight crew members from the *Strathblane* escaped on a small boat attached to the ship. The *Strathblane* began to turn on its side and to split apart. Some of the men started swimming toward the distant land. The captain decided to go down with his ship. Seven people drowned and 22 survived.

# Cape Disappointment Light Still Shines

Cape D still lights the way for ships. In 1962, the lighthouse became **automated.** This means it operates on its own, without keepers. The light now runs on electricity and has a brightness of 160,000 candlepower. There is a U.S. Coast Guard station at Cape Disappointment. This station has special **equipment** to help ships cross the sandbar safely. The lighthouse itself is not open to the public, but visitors can take a short, steep hike up to Cape Disappointment Light. Cape D has one of the most breathtaking views on the West Coast.

*Cape D has helped to save many lives.*

# Glossary

**ancient** (AYN-chent)  Very old, from a long time ago.

**automated** (AW-tuh-mayt-ed)  When something operates on its own, without help.

**balcony** (BAL-kuh-nee)  A platform that sticks out from the outside of a building.

**candlepower** (KAN-duhl-pow-uhr)  The amount of light coming from one candle.

**Congress** (KON-gres)  The part of the U.S. government that makes laws.

**current** (KUR-ent)  The flow of water in a certain direction.

**daymarker** (DAY-mark-er)  A lighthouse with a special color scheme or pattern that identifies it during the daytime.

**distress** (dih-STREHS)  To be in danger.

**equipment** (uh-KWIP-mint)  All the supplies needed to do an activity.

**installed** (in-STAHLD)  To have been set up for use.

**navigation** (nah-vuh-GAY-shun)  A way of figuring out which way a ship is headed.

**order** (OR-der)  The size of the Fresnel lens that determines the brightness and the distance that light will travel.

**port** (PORT)  A place where ships can dock or anchor safely.

**rod** (ROD)  A thin, straight piece of metal.

**routes** (ROOTS)  The paths that people take to get somewhere.

**stranded** (STRAND-ed)  To be left alone in a hard situation.

**surveyors** (sur-VAY-erz)  People who measure or find areas of land to build on.

**treacherous** (TREH-chuh-rus)  Full of danger.

**wicks** (WIHKS)  Cords in lamps or in candles that soak up fuel and burn when lit.

# Index

**A**
Alexandria, Egypt, 5

**C**
Columbia River, 6, 9,
     13, 21

**D**
daymarker, 14

**E**
Esterbrook, George, 18

**F**
fog bell, 14

Fresnel, Augustin, 17
Fresnel lens, 17

**G**
gold, 10

**H**
Heceta, Bruno, 9

**K**
keepers, 18, 21–22

**M**
Meares, John, 9
Munson, Joel, 18

**O**
Oregon Territory, 10
*Oriole*, 13

**P**
Pacific Ocean, 6, 13
Pharos, 5

**S**
sandbar, 6, 13,
     21–22
*Strathblane*, 21

**U**
U.S. Coast Guard, 22

# Web Sites

To learn more about Cape Disappointment Light, check out these Web sites:
http://travelthecoast.com/pelicanpost/article_lighthouses.asp
www.pbs.org/legendarylighthouses/html/pnwwagl.html